D0118780

at home with ...

The Ancient Romans

...in history

BROWN BEAR BOOKS

Published by Brown Bear Books Ltd
4877 N. Circulo Bujia
Tucson, AZ 85718
USA

and

First Floor
9-17 St. Albans Place
London N1 0NX

© 2014 Brown Bear Books Ltd

ISBN–13: 978-1-78121-082-6

All rights reserved. No part of this book may
be reproduced, stored in a retrieval system, or
transmitted in any form or by any means, electronic,
mechanical, photocopying, recording, or otherwise,
without the prior written permission of the copyright
holder.

Library of Congress Cataloging-in-Publication Data
available upon request

Author: Tim Cooke
Designer: Lynne Lennon
Picture manager: Sophie Mortimer
Design manager: Keith Davis
Editorial director: Lindsey Lowe
Children's publisher: Anne O'Daly

Printed in the United States of America

AG/5530
04/2014

Websites
The website addresses (URLs) included in this book were
valid at the time of going to press. However, because of
the nature of the internet, it is possible that some addresses
may have changed, or sites may have changed or closed
down since publication. While the author and publisher
regret any inconvenience this may cause the readers, no
responsibility for any such changes can be accepted by
either the author or the publisher.

Picture credits
Key: b = bottom, bgr = background, c = centre, is = insert,
l = left, mtg = montage, r = right, t = top.

Front Cover: Shutterstock: l; **Thinkstock:** istockphoto
main, tr:
Interior: Alamy: Erin Babnik 29r, Heritage Image
Partnership Ld 28; **De Agostini Picture Library:** 24;
Getty Images: The Bridgeman Art Library 23b; **RHL:** 15l,
16tr, 21r,27; Louvre, Paris 22r; **Shutterstock:** 8, 11b,16b, 21
ADA Photos 25t, Alessandro 23t, Olag Babich 26,
Benedictus 7b, S. Borisov 7t, Claudio Divizia 27tr,
Eric Isselee 25cr, Melissa King 17l,Vladimir Korostyshevskiy
29l, Pius Lee 11t, Mountainpix 21cl, Steven Wright 5t;
Thinkstock: istockphoto 4, 6, 10,14,15br,17t,18,18-19b,
Photos.com 12; **Topfoto:** 5b, Fine Art Images/Heritage
Images 13t.

All other artworks Brown Bear Books.

Brown Bear Books has made every attempt to contact the
copyright holder. If you have any information please contact
licensing@brownbearbooks.co.uk

Contents

We CAME, we SAW, we **CONQUERED**
... And then we went HOME to eat **stuffed DORMICE**

Welcome to Rome!

What do you know about ancient Rome?
Probably that gladiators fought in the arena. Maybe that the
emperors were superpowerful. Or that Hadrian built a wall in
northern Britain. And probably that the Romans loved to go to
the baths. Right?

Well, none of that is WRONG,
but it's only PART of the story.
We're going to take you behind the scenes.

Hot facts

 Rome stands on the Tiber River in what is now Italy.

 It first became powerful in around 500 B.C.E. The Romans formed a republic and gradually took over the rest of Italy.

 Roman power also spread around the Mediterranean to North Africa.

 In 31 B.C.E., Octavian became the sole ruler. He called himself Augustus Caesar. This marked the beginning of the empire.

 The republic was ruled by elected consuls. The most famous was Julius Caesar.

* KILLING GROUND! *
Arena used for over 500 years for gladiator fights and animal hunts!

WE RULE THE WORLD

Top Dogs in Europe

Roman Boast!

Not all Romans came from Rome. At the height of the Roman empire, men all over Europe and North Africa could proudly claim *Civis Romanus sum*—"I am a citizen of Rome."

- The emperors built huge public buildings in Rome to show off their power.
- The Roman Empire reached its greatest extent under Emperor Trajan in 117 C.E.
- Rome began to decline as its enemies began to take back land from the empire.
- In 330, the Emperor Constantine built a second capital at Constantinople (now Istanbul in Turkey).
- In 395, the Roman Empire was split into a western half, ruled from Rome, and an eastern half, ruled from Constantinople.
- In 476, a Germanic army attacked Rome and deposed the final emperor, Romulus Augustus.

Big in the CITY!

Getting Here

Do you know the phrase "All roads lead to Rome?" Well, they do. A huge network of straight, paved roads joins all parts of the empire to the capital. They're by far the quickest way to travel overland.

You've never seen anything like Rome. Over a million people live here. It's hard to imagine, but as recently as the eighth century B.C.E., it was still just a couple of villages. Nine hundred years later, Rome is the biggest city in the world.

Up and Down

Bring your walking sandals!

Rome is built on seven hills. They're the hills where the original farming peoples lived beside the Tiber River. When the tribes began to get together for religious rituals, they decided to merge their settlements. In the fourth century B.C.E., the emperor Severus enclosed the seven hills with a wall that set the city's first boundary.

LIQUID ENGINEERING

Rome has clean running water in all the public fountains and bathhouses (although not in private houses). Aqueducts carry fresh water from springs in the countryside—and all by the force of gravity. If that's not enough of an engineering marvel for you, check out the spectacular bridges that carry aqueducts over valleys, like this one near Nimes in France.

not sure **which** **GOD** is the best?

Rome has so many gods and goddesses, it's sometimes difficult to know which one to turn to. Well, that doesn't have to be a problem. Now Romans can worship them all at the same time in the Pantheon. This spectacular temple was built in 126 C.E. to honor all the gods and goddesses of Rome.

In the **Hood**

Everyone except the very rich lives in insulae. These "islands" are apartment buildings six or seven stories high.

✻ Don't live too high up. The best apartments are lower down. And upstairs it's harder to get out if there is a fire.

✻ Insulae have shops and businesses at ground level. Avoid living above a tanner's: they stink!

✻ Beware of bad landlords. Skinflints build tenements very cheaply—so they often collapse.

Rome's **Port**

Take a trip to Ostia. Rome's port is only 19 miles (30 km) down the Tiber. Ships arrive from everywhere carrying everything. Check out the granaries, the lighthouse, and the theater. Ride back on a barge carrying grain to Rome. The government makes sure Romans have enough grain for bread—otherwise, there's a danger of a riot!

Ostia's lighthouse is FAMOUS for being so TALL

The Big Drain

A million people generate a lot of ... waste. Around 600 B.C.E., one of the world's first sewage systems was built to drain waste into the Tiber. Waste from public bathrooms (ordinary homes have cesspits) runs into the Cloaca Maxima, the "Big Drain." After you've used the communal lavatories, why not visit the spot where the drain runs into the river (but make sure to hold your nose!).

Rome:
THINGS to DO

What's happening in Rome? There's something for everyone. But be warned: Most of it is not for the squeamish. Most people start with the great arenas: the Colosseum (below) or the Circus Maximus.

Around town

Hot list

1 ★ **Executions** It's always worth passing by the base of the Tarpeian Rock in case a traitor or murderer is being thrown off the 80-foot (25-m) cliff.

2 ★ **Chariots** There's racing at the Circus Maximus 66 days a year, with champions from all over the empire. Watch 24 races a day!

3 ★ **Animals** A Libyan has trained elephants to write! Watch them spell in the sand with their trunks!

4 ★ **Gladiators** Choose from solo or team contests, or even animals vs. animals. Look out for elephants vs. rhinos: a classic matchup!

5 ★ **Drama** There's always a good play on. Try the comedies of Plautus or the dramas of Seneca. All the stories are based on the best Greek originals.

6 ★ **Naval battle** Watch Rome's galleys in battle! See the Colosseum flooded with water (it's 5 feet [1.5 m] deep and takes seven hours to fill).

Hits and **misses:** ✔ We **LOVED** Plautus's new comedy *Baccharia*. Great **MASKS!**

CHARIOT RACES

On race days, visit the Circus Maximus. It's free—and there are 250,000 seats. Try to get a seat at either end of the track, where the chariots make a U-turn. That's where you'll see the biggest crashes—and even deaths. Dress well: The emperor might be there.

Show of skill
The best charioteers race with four horses rather than two—that's too easy!

MAN AGAINST BEAST

If you're bored of the usual fights or you don't want to see Christians torn apart, watch gladiators fight animals for a change. Tigers, lions, elephants, bears: There's lots of choice. But the gladiators are usually well armed, so it's not really a fair fight!

Classic contest
The short sword vs. the net and trident is an old favorite.

GLADIATORS   WILD ANIMALS   CHRISTIANS

79   6   0

Meet

Maximus Dangerus

Q. Maximus, what do you think about today's contests?
A. I hope they'll go our way.

Q. Don't they always go your way? You gladiators killed 5,000 animals last time.
A. True, we are well armed—but the animals are still dangerous.

Q. What are you fighting today? Lions? Hippos?
A. Um, it's a bit embarrassing.

Q. Don't be embarrassed.
A. I'm fighting a giraffe.

Q. Wow, that really is embarrassing.
A. It wasn't my idea, honest! The emperor wants to see it.

What's Maximus Dangerus doing—??! That's just **IDIOTIC!** Fighting a **GIRAFFE**. That takes some neck!!

In the **service of** the *Empire*

Under the Emperor Trajan, our Roman empire has grown bigger than ever before (and in fact, bigger than it will ever be again). So where are the best places to visit?

You're welcome! Gaps in Hadrian's Wall allow traders in. Buy some of their blue woad!

Scotland ✗

It's cold and rainy a lot of the time. There are no cities to stay in. The local Picts are not very welcoming. In fact, they're so unwelcoming that the Emperor Hadrian built a fortified wall to keep them out! Only soldiers go here—and they take spare pairs of thick socks.

TOURIST RATING ☀
For the specialist only

Constantinople ✓

The capital of the empire in the east is named after Emperor Constantine. He plunked it there in the fourth century C.E. on top of an old Greek city named Byzantium. It guards the narrow strait between the Mediterranean and the Black Sea. Just across the strait is Asia! Constantine's ambitious building plans made Constantinople the new Rome. Be sure to visit its many Christian basilicas, or churches.

TOURIST RATING ☀ ☀ ☀ ☀
Home away from home!

Also worth a **look:** ✓ Hispania (**SPAIN**): We especially love the aqueduct in Segovia.

Libya ❌

Head for Leptis Magna or the boom town of Ghirza. You're almost guaranteed good weather in North Africa. But be warned. This is a rich region, because of all the grain it sends to Rome. You'll find everything pricey.

TOURIST RATING ✳
A rip-off!

Wise Sphinx
The Romans thought the Sphinx might guard a library of ancient knowledge

Egypt ✅

From the moment you sail past the lighthouse at Pharos into the port of Alexandria, you're guaranteed a great time. Bring home sacred water from the Nile River. See the glistening white pyramids (the limestone covering will fall off eventually). Visit an embalming shop to see mummies being made. Or go the whole hog and book to be mummified yourself (when you're dead, of course).

TOURIST RATING ✳ ✳ ✳ ✳ *Something for everyone!*

The Rhine ❌

It's the edge of the empire. Beyond the Rhine River live Germanic tribes who don't like Rome. They're always raiding across the barriers—and they are getting bolder. The poor security situation means this is strictly for the military.

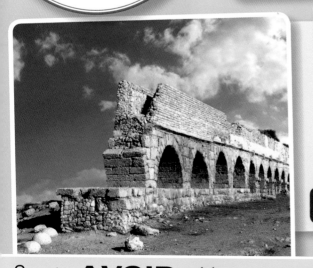

Judea ✅

Caesarea Maritima is the provincial capital. It was built by the governor Herod. You might have heard of him. He sentenced all baby boys to death to try to kill a Christian prophet named Moses. (He failed.) His city has a fine aqueduct and a busy harbor. And lots of desert sand.

TOURIST RATING ✳ ✳ ✳ *A triumph*

One to **AVOID:** ❌ **POMPEII** in Campania is popular—but **WHAT ABOUT** that volcano next door?

coming of the EMPERORS

It's no secret. You don't have to be crazy to rule Rome—but it might help! We've had some pretty nutty emperors. Some good, some bad—and some just plain insane.

👎 **Tiberius 14–37**: *Too lazy*
He let his guards run the empire while he spent his time living in luxury on the island of Capri.
Fate: Died of old age.

👎 **Caligula 37–41**: *Way too cruel*
Killed anyone who disagreed with him. Declared himself a god. Tried to make his horse, Incitatus, a consul. Tortured his enemies to death. Once ordered spectators at the Colosseum to be thrown to the lions.
Fate: Stabbed to death by the Praetorian Guard and left for dogs to eat.

👎 **Nero 54–68**: *Too crazy*
Had anyone close to him executed, including his mother, Agrippina, and his second wife, Poppaea. Imposed huge taxes to pay for his luxury lifestyle. Was said to have played his lyre during a terrible fire that destroyed Rome—but that's not actually true.
Fate: Killed himself after being sentenced to death.

👎 **Domitian 81–96**: *Too cruel*
Persecuted foreign religions, especially Christians and Jews.
Fate: Stabbed to death by conspirators.

Self-important
Nero killed himself with the words, "What an artist dies in me!"

The **WORST** emperors ... the **roll call** of **SHAME**

Commodus 180–192: *Too distracted*
Commodus fought in the arena, even though he was emperor and the gladiators were slaves. He even forced beggars to fight each other to death in the Colosseum.
Fate: Strangled in the bath by his favorite gladiator by order of the Senate.

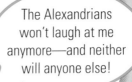
The Alexandrians won't laugh at me anymore—and neither will anyone else!

 Caracalla 198–217: *Too violent*
Executed his brother (and co-emperor) Geta and Geta's wife. When the citizens of Alexandria in Egypt made fun of this action in a play, Caracalla led an army to Egypt and killed 20,000 Alexandrians in the town square.
Fate: Stabbed by his own guards as he peed by the side of the road.

 Elagabalus 218–222: *Too confused!*
Asked doctors to discover how they could turn him into a woman. Then he married a Vestal Virgin—that's a big no-no.
Fate: Stabbed to death, beheaded, and thrown into the Tiber River.

 Maximinus Thrax 235–238:
Too aggressive
Kept invading Rome's peaceful neighbors—Germany, Ukraine, and Romania—until even the army had had enough of his wars.
Fate: Stabbed and beheaded by the Praetorian Guard.

Diocletian 284–305

Too horrible! Started the idea of throwing Christians to the lions, after the oracle of the god Apollo told him to persecute them.
Fate: Suicide after a peaceful retirement.

Uneven fight
Christian martyrs pray as the wild beasts are released into the arena.

Get the LOOK!

Get your glad rags out! The Romans like to dress in their best clothes for all kinds of occasions. But watch your purse—fashion changes quickly, and keeping up can be very expensive.

Look Stylish!

Romans like to look their best whenever they go out: to a dinner party, to the Circus, or to the Colosseum. Everyone makes a special effort for an event where the emperor might be present.

the colour PURPLE

It's easy to recognize important people in Rome. They're the ones wearing purple. The more purple, the more important. (If their robes are all purple, they're probably a god—so be polite!) The purple dye comes from tiny mollusks from Phoenicia. It costs a fortune. That's why purple is the color of senators and emperors.

Fashion Tip

Rules and Regulations

Romans can't just wear what they want. Their clothes have to show their place in society. Regulations called sumptuary laws stop people from spending too much on clothes.

★ No purple dye, apart from aristocrats and rulers.

★ No silk for men—too sissy!

★ Togas are only for adult males.

★ Limited numbers of stripes to be woven on togas.

★ No pants, ever—they're too "barbarian," because they come from Scythia, outside the empire.

Hits and misses: ✔ We LOVED the new pleated KILTS for the army—Ideal for fighting!

get those **ruffles**

Ladies! Rethink your stola. We've been wearing these Greek ankle-length tunics for centuries, gathered at the waist. Vary the shape by using buttons on the arms to make sleeves of various lengths. Add a colored fringe or a band of gold embroidery. Let a long stola sweep behind you in a train, or gather it in ruffles behind your bottom. And try swapping dreary wool for bright linen or cotton. But watch out for colored silk: It's so thin, it's see through!

Fancy sleeves
The Ionic style of stola uses buttons to vary the length of the sleeve.

Drag along
Style victims let their stolas drag behind them on the ground.

Fancy fringe
Dress up your stola with a fringe of blue, red, yellow or gold.

Stylewatch

What's with the toga?

The toga is a simple piece of cloth about 20 feet (6 meters) long draped around the body. It can be worn in a variety of ways. There are eight main styles. The most common is plain white. But it's only for men and only for citizens—no slaves or foreigners allowed.

Shoes and Sandals

Everyone loves shoes—and Rome has the best. If you're a slave, you'll wear the *carabatina*, a leather sandal. Citizens wear the *calceus*, which closes over the whole foot (you'll have to learn to tie your shoelaces). For indoors, there are house sandals. Soldiers have boots up to the knees or hobnailed *caliga* for marching. And who can forget the red high heels worn by Julius Caesar? He said they were a sign of royalty—and soon, all the aristocrats were wearing them.

Royal footsteps
Caesar claims the old Etruscan kings wore red high heels.

Creation of Felt

Our old friend Saint Clement claims to have come up with a great new invention. Setting out on a long hike, he placed pieces of wool inside his leather sandals. But after days of walking in the heat, his sweaty feet had pressed the wool into a new type of material. We call it felt.

✖ A merchant in the Forum was caught wearing red sandals. **NO! NO! NO!** Red is for **aristocrats**, not for the **PLEBS!**

Keeping up
Appearances

Any Roman except the very poorest takes a lot of pride in how he or she looks. It's not just a question of clothes. Makeup and hair are on everyone's mind. Getting ready to go out takes ages.

A makeup **cabinet** for every **woman**

We Romans very rarely go out without makeup. This basic selection will allow every woman to achieve the latest looks.

Fucus   red paint for coloring the cheeks and lips

Wood ash   for black eyeshadow

Saffron   for gold eyeshadow

Antimony   to darken the eyelids and eyebrows

Blue paint   to outline your veins

Sheep's fat   to color fingernails

Pumice stone   to whiten teeth

Saliva (from a slave) to help make a paste to apply the fucus

Makeup was not thought appropriate for the young

Poppaea's beauty **Tips**

The wife of the Emperor Nero, Poppaea Sabina, is the empire's most stylish woman. Here are some of her beauty secrets.

★ **Asses' milk**. This is my number 1 essential. I bathe in it to keep my skin soft. I also soak bread in it, to make a paste that I put on my face overnight. It's dreamy!

★ **Color.** I cover my face with white lead and then color my lips and cheeks red, for a highlight.

★ **Beauty marks**. I stick these little black crescent shapes, called plenia, all over my face as beauty spots.

★ **Slaves**. Yes, I know they're a luxury, but I use 100 slaves to help me dress in my transparent stolas of blue, yellow, green, and pink.

Makeover magic: ✔ Get your **PORTRAIT BUST** carved with detachable hair that you can upda

What's that smell?

Want to avoid the effects of aging? Think poo. Not just any poo, but the poo of a crocodile. You should be able to pick it up from a trader in Rome. Ask for imported poo from Egypt or Libya. For a full-body treatment, mix the poo with mud to fill a bathtub. Or apply as a face mask just before bed and leave on overnight. (But remember to wash if off in the morning.)

Blondes ...
Do they really have more fun?

Since barbarian slaves with fair hair started turning up in Rome after wars in the empire, Roman women have tried to get the new look. Some bleach their hair with henna. Wealthy women dust their hair with powder made from real gold or silver. And some take a direct approach. They just cut off the slaves' blonde hair and use it to make wigs.

Dye damage
Some women caused so much damage lightening their hair, they had to wear wigs!

AT THE BARBER

Men—don't cut your own hair at home. Try the barber shop. They're the first anywhere in the world. Barbers are always busy with gossiping men waiting on benches to have their hair cut or waved and covered in perfume. A boy's first haircut is recorded in city hall.

Barbers do shaves, too. A senator isn't allowed to take his seat in the Senate if he hasn't shaved first.

What's with **OVID?** The poet loves to whine about the rapid change of **FASHION** and **HAIRSTYLES**. Get with it, man!

17

at the Baths

We Romans love keeping clean more than any other people. Whenever we conquer new territory, we find a hot spring and build a bathhouse. It's not just to keep clean: Hanging out at the baths is a whole lot of fun!

Splish Splash—HOW to take a perfect bath

★ Make sure you have some time. A good bath can't be rushed.
★ Give your clothes to the attendant and head to the palaestra (gymnasium).
★ Do some exercise to work up a sweat.
★ Head for the tepidarium (warm room) to get used to the heat.

Dos and don'ts: ✔ If you take **SERVANTS** to the **BATHS**, make them use the **BACK DOO**

A Palace for Pleasure!

Welcome to the Baths of Diocletian. It's 600 years since the first bathhouse was built in around 300 B.C.E., and this is the most sensational yet. The new baths are huge. They can easily fit 3,000 people at the same time. There's a hot room used as a sauna; a huge cold room with a plunge pool; a swimming pool; massage rooms; gyms for exercising; libraries; lecture rooms; and a garden. If you're shy, ask for a private bathing box.

Crime Wave!

Everyone knows about the baths at Aquae Sulis (Bath, in England). They stand on a hot spring that the Celts saw as sacred. But now bathers there are facing a serious problem. They keep having their clothes stolen. More than 130 people have thrown curse tablets into the baths. The tiny sheets of lead have curses scratched into them asking the gods to punish the thieves.

Noisy Bathers!

The playwright Seneca is complaining about the baths near his home. He says the grunting and slapping of massages puts him off. How can he work when people are talking loudly or splashing in the pool?

Aromatic oils

There's no soap, so take along oil scented with herbs or with spices from Asia.

★ **Face the real heat:** Take a sauna in the caldarium (hot room).
★ **Find a masseur** to rub scented olive oil all over you (no one uses soap); they'll then scrape off the oil and sweat.
★ **Plunge** into the cold bath in the frigidarium (cold room).
★ **Take a swim** in the pool; find your friends and hang out.

✖ Don't go to the baths with a **fresh WOUND**—you might get an **INFECTION** from the **dirt!**

Welcome **to my** Beautiful *Home*

Everyone who is everyone has a villa—and everyone who is not anyone works for them! These luxurious country houses have large estates attached. Slaves grow fruit, grapes, grain, honey, or olives.

What to look for in a villa:

Cool kitchen
It's good to have all the latest gadgets, even if the cooking is done by slaves, not by you!

A BUYER'S GUIDE

- Be private! Your villa should just have one or two doors, so they are easy to lock for security. And no outside windows—you don't want snoopers looking in.
- Make sure your villa is built around at least one atrium. This open courtyard will keep the rest of the house cool.

It should have a pool or fountain (the water helps cool the air) and a covered portico for shade in bright sunshine.
- The bedrooms should be quiet. Make sure they're not too close to the kitchen!
- On the ground floor, there should be offices for the master to do business.
- The best villas have two dining rooms, for the summer and winter.

Home DECORATION: ✔ We **LOVE** the sound of the Villa Romana del Casale on Sicily.

CENTRAL HEATING

If your villa is in a cooler part of the empire, avoid getting chilly with a hypocaust. This hollow space beneath floors and in the walls fills with hot air from a furnace fed by slaves. The underfloor heating warms the rooms. (Save money by using the steam for your private bathhouse, too.)

Dinner Guest
Put a statue of the Lares at the table during dinner, to make sure of their blessing.

Dizzying Decoration

Bare concrete or plaster is so five years ago. Gung-ho owners are adorning their properties with complex mosaic floors. They might be geometric shapes, or they might illustrate real scenes. These pictures made from pieces of colored clay take ages to make, so they're very expensive. Or try a wall painting. A skilled fresco artist will recreate a whole rural scene for you—perhaps even a view of your own estate.

Household gods!

Never forget the household gods. These Lares look after your villa. Pray at your Lararium, or shrine, every day—and don't forget to make small offerings of food. The Lares love that!

It has more **MOSAICS** than any other villa! They include famous images of **young WOMEN** playing sports.

21

a LIFE of LUXURY!

The best way to enjoy Rome was to be rich—very rich. And some Romans became very wealthy as the economy boomed.

Early EMPIRE **Booming!**
Riches of the **Republic** Continue!

Money continues to flow into the city since the end of the Republic. Tribute and taxes arrive from all over the empire. Trade and banking make huge profits. After every victory in war, loot from the defeated enemy adds to Rome's fortune. It's a great time to make money! Politicians use this wealth to buy the people's support, so that they can get elected to positions of power. They also spend it on new buildings and on paying great artists and craftsmen.

All Hail
Marcus Licinius Crassus

It's official! Crassus is the richest man in the Republic. We all know his talent as a general. He defeated the slave rebellion led by Spartacus. But it's Crassus' sideline in property dealing that has made him so rich. When he became a consul in 70 B.C.E., he fed the population of Rome at 10,000 tables—and gave them enough grain for three months.

> I even charge people to use my own private fire department.

Not built in a day!
Each emperor added temples and other buildings to the glory of Rome.

Live in **style:** ✔ Say goodbye to drafts. Get some **GLASS** in your windows. It's not just for jewelry!

Maritime Theater
This circular portico held up by pillars contains a ring-shaped pool and an island.

Retreat
This house was Hadrian's retreat on the island.

Connections
Originally, the island was connected to the banks by drawbridges.

Cut-Price Luxury

We're all used to wearing cameos as jewelry. But these brooches carved in layers of glass are so expensive. Now that the empire is growing poorer, try substituting cheaper mosaic glass for cameo glass. For other ways to save money, use marbled tableware instead of agate. And try making jewelry out of gold coins. Since the inflation of the third century B.C.E., it's hardly worth using as money anymore!

Meet
Emperor Hadrian

Q. Emperor Hadrian, what can you tell us about your new villa?
A.It's just outside Rome. It has a garden and about 30 buildings. The most important is my palace, but I also have baths, temples, a theater, libraries, and places to run the government.

Q. Isn't it a little overindulgent?
A. How dare you question the emperor? But you're right. I suppose I do like to surround myself with fine artworks. A lot of them are from Greece. And I like being outside the city. It's less stressful.

Q. What are your favorite parts of the villa?
A. I like the Canopus, a pool surrounded by Greek columns.

Q. Where do you get your ideas for buildings?
A. From my travels. That's why you'll see Greek and Egyptian architecture here, together with Roman-style buildings.

Q. And who do you think will enjoy your villa most?
A. What an odd question! Me, of course. It's not for anyone else to enjoy!

Don't copy Hadrian and fill your **HOUSE** with **STATUES**. Once you die, all your friends will just **PINCH** them!

Come to Dinner!

Food, food, and more food: Romans love to eat anything, from songbirds to whole pigs. Can't decide? Why not bake the songbirds inside the pig and enjoy both at the same time!

Eat lying down!

We've got a great night lined up for wealthy guests: food, food, … and more food. There'll be three courses at dinner, so bring along your own napkin and spoon. You can take off your sandals and lie back on one of the three couches around the table. We can promise you deep philosophical conversation—and lots of fascinating gossip. Later, there will be music and a mime performance. Oh, and some more food.

Food day: ✔ Everyone eats **BREAKFAST** at dawn, a **SNACK** around 11:00 A.M., and **dinner** at night.

I'm Not Eating THAT!

The problem with edible snails is that they're always trying to escape. Our tip: Keep them on an artificial island surrounded by water. Feed them on milk until they're too fat to fit back into their shells. Then fry them and serve with some tasty fish sauce. Delicious!

Or THAT!

There isn't much meat on a dormouse. So buy a special pot with rooms and pathways where they live while you fatten them up. Once they are fat enough, simply roast the dormice inside the pot. To make an even tastier snack, stuff the mice with pork and pine nuts, or dip them in honey.

Don't eat me, I'm too cute!

Fattening Up
Feed your edible dormice on walnuts, chestnuts, or acorns for a nutty taste.

And DEFINITELY Not THAT!

Everyone loves garum, but do you know how this famous fish sauce is made? The intestines of fish are removed and placed in a bowl, covered in salt, and then left in the sun. The sun's heat makes the fish guts ferment, and the clear liquid that rises to the top is sieved off to form garum. It might have some herbs added, but its main flavor is a savory mix of fish and salt. TOO savory for some!

Liquid lunch
Amphorae are essential. These clay containers hold oil, wine, and other liquids.

WHOOPS!

We're sad to report the death of the gourmet Marcus Gavius Apicius. He took his love of cooking too far. His famous kitchen cost 100 million sesterces. But when he realized that the work had left him nearly broke, he was so upset that he took his own life.

Spare wood
Cook over a wood fire—pine logs give a nice taste.

✖ Don't try the **GREEK** way: breakfast, a second **breakfast** at noon and **DINNER** in the **AFTERNOON**! CRAZY!

25

At the MARKET

Rome is the heart of the Mediterranean economy. Goods flow in from all over the world. The citizens can buy virtually anything they want—as long as they've got the money!

The forum is the heart of public life in Rome

Imports

* If you've got the money, we can get it for you! Our merchants will go to the ends of the Earth to get what you want.

Today's specials:

- TIN from Britain
- colored SILKS from China
- COTTON from Egypt or India
- perfumed OILS from India (great for the bathhouse!)
- FRANKINCENSE and MYRRH from Arabia and East Africa
- SPICES from Southeast Asia
- IVORY from Egypt

AT THE FORUM

Whatever you need, head for the forum. Every town and city has one of these open squares. Rome has lots, each specializing in products such as meat or vegetables. You'll find tabernae, or stores, around the outside. The large basilica will hold more stores, plus the offices of lawyers and accountants. Or head for the stalls lining the stoa, or covered walkway. The forum is the center of public life. It's always busy. You never know who you might meet. But keep your hands on your purse—there are always thieves around!

Grab yourself a **bargain:** ✔ While stocks last! Fresh **GRAIN** from Egypt and North Africa

Prices **Soar!**

What's going on with the sesterces? Since the empire stopped growing in the second century C.E., prices have gone up and up. There's less gold coming into Rome, so there's less gold to make coins. Coins with less gold are worth less, so merchants put up their prices. Things have gotten so bad that some people have stopped using money completely. They barter, or exchange goods for other goods, instead.

Trajan's Treasure
Trajan's Market is built on a number of different levels linked by staircases

Trajan's **MARKET**

Emperor Trajan has opened the world's first shopping center. Or has he? No one is quite sure what the building is for. From the front, it looks like it has semicircular rows of shops—but none have goods entrances in the back. So maybe it's just more offices, after all.

A NOTE FROM THE AEDILE

I, Julius Caesar, am proud to be your new aedile. It's one of my jobs to protect you from cheating merchants. That's why I insist that traders use standard measures and weights. Take the amphora, a measure of liquid. It's based on a jug called the amphora capitolina—which is so important, it's kept in the Temple of Jupiter in the Capitoline Hill in Rome.

Whenever you're shopping, make sure the merchant has a license to trade. It's carved in marble and should be on display at the front of the store. It's my guarantee to you that it's safe to shop.

✖ Don't want to carry your shopping home? All decent women use a **SLAVE** to do the **DONKEYWORK!**

27

You can't
Get the HELP

The Roman Empire may be the greatest power in the world—but it relies on lots of people doing some terrible jobs.

Wanted

Gladiator

Some gladiators get to be heroes and make a fortune. But most don't. They live as slaves, they train to fight in arenas all over the empire—and they keep on fighting until they eventually get killed. Sometimes they even have to fight their own friends.

Vomit Collector

Roman dinner parties always need a special slave to clean up the vomit after guests have thrown up. Lovely!

Soothsayer

Everyone listens to an augur before taking a decision, so augurs are very respected. They read the will of the gods … in animal entrails. They cut animals open and study their insides. They burn the remains and read the flames. Then they make their prediction. Woe betide them if they give the emperor bad advice.

Galley Slave

Roman galleys [boats] have up to 25 pairs of oars, each of which has up to three rowers. The most skilled man sets the speed of rowing. The other two are untrained convicts or slaves who follow his time. The oarsmen sit in rows on wooden benches. Bring a cushion—and water to drink!

Job **Advice:** ✔ **MATH** is a useful skill for getting a job as an **ENGINEER** or **SURVEYOR**.

Skin Scraper

It's hot and sweaty work. When Romans want to get clean, they rub scented olive oil into their skin, then get themselves sweaty in the heat of the baths. A slave then uses a small, curved metal strigil to scrape the oil and dirt off the skin—all over the body. This is definitely not a job for someone embarrassed by naked flesh!

Slave Society

Being a slave is never much fun. But some slaves have a better life than others. They don't make fires, clean the floor, or dig the fields. They run entire households—and enjoy a lot of privileges.

Sisterhood

For 1,000 years, the six Vestal Virgins were superpowerful in Roman religion.

Pick your tool

Strigils come in different sizes to scrape different parts of the body.

Multitasker

The same slaves who scrape off the oil often also give massages.

Vestal Virgins

To become a priestess of the Goddess Vesta, apply before the age of 10. You'll have to agree to have no boyfriends for 30 years. You'll also have to leave your family and live in Vesta's temple. You'll have many privileges—but you might also be punished. If you let the sacred fire of Vesta go out, you'll be whipped. And if you do have a boyfriend, you'll be buried alive—with just enough food and water to make sure you suffer horribly for a few days.

Don't put up with a **POOR** salary. Convince your fellow workers to go on **STRIKE** for more money!

29

Glossary

aedile An elected official who was responsible for public works and games, and who supervised markets.

agate A kind of stone used to make jewelry.

amphora A two-handled jar with a narrow neck that the Romans used to store liquids such as oil and wine.

aqueduct A channel that is designed to move water over long distances, usually by the power of gravity.

atrium An open-roofed courtyard or entrance hall in a Roman house.

augur An official who foretold the future by observing signs and omens.

basilica A large building originally used in Rome for public meetings or trials.

cameo A gem or shell carved with a raised design.

consul One of the chief magistrates of Rome. Two consuls were elected for a term of one year.

empire A group of countries that are ruled by an emperor or empress.

gladiator A professional fighter or prisoner who fought in public tournaments.

Lararium A small household shrine devoted to the Lares of a home.

Lares The household gods that looked after a home.

mosaic A picture or design made out of small pieces of colored stone.

plebians (or plebs) The name for the common people of ancient Rome.

persecute To ill-treat a part of society. usually because of their religion or race.

portico A roof or porch supported by columns.

Praetorian Guard The emperor's bodyguards.

republic A political system in which voters elect a group of politicians to represent them.

sesterce An ancient Roman coin.

strait A narrow channel of water joining two large bodies of water.

sumptuary law A regulation that prevents people from spending too much money on their clothes or lifestyle.

Vestal Virgin A priestess in the temple of the goddess Vesta.

On the Web

www.pbs.org/empires/romans/empire/life.html
Site to accompany the PBS TV series *The Roman Empire in the First Century*.

www.history.com/topics/ancient_rome
The History Channel site with photos, videos, and information about ancient Rome.

http://ed.ted.com/lessons/a-glimpse-of-teenage-life-in-ancient-rome-ray-laurence
A short video lesson about Roman life from Ted.com.

www.kidinfo.com/world_history/ancient_rome.html
Excellent site with links related to all aspects of life in ancient Rome, from clothes and chariots to art, architecture, and mythology.

Books

Catel, Patrick. *What Did the Ancient Romans Do For Me?* Heinemann Library, 2011.

Deary, Terry. *Ruthless Romans* (Horrible Histories). Scholastic, 2012.

Dubois, Muriel L. *Ancient Rome: A Mighty Empire* (Fact Finders: Great Civilizations). Capstone Press, 2011.

Hanel, Rachael. *Ancient Rome: An Interactive History Adventure* (You Choose: Historical Eras). You Choose Books, 2010.

Holm, Kirsten. *Everyday Life in Ancient Rome* (Junior Graphic Ancient Civilizations). Powerkids Press, 2012.

James, Simon. *Ancient Rome* (DK Eyewitness Books). DK Children, 2008.

James, Simon. *Eyewitness: Ancient Rome*. Dorling Kindersley, 2008.

Malay, John. *You Wouldn't Want to Be a Roman Gladiator!: Gory Things You'd Rather Not Know*. Franklin Watts, 2012.

Index